# A HONITON LACE

The Pat Perryman Story

by

Trevor Hitchcock BA

Published by:

The Allhallows Museum Society of Honiton
High Street
Honiton
Devon
EX14 1PG

Telephone: 01404 44966

e-mail: info@honitonmuseum.co.uk
Website: www.honitonmuseum.co.uk

Registered Charity No. 306645    Accredited Museum No. RD798

© 2009 Trevor Hitchcock / The Allhallows Museum Society of Honiton

Printed by Besley and Copp, Exeter, Devon

**ISBN: 978-0-9554238-1-9**

*Pat, aged 11, in her new Guide uniform with her twin sisters Valerie and Carol in Brownie uniform.     Photographer: Harry Holton.*

# A Honiton Lace Maker.

Lace making has been a traditional craft in and around Honiton for over 450 years. Believed to have been introduced to the East Devon area by refugees from the 16$^{th}$ century religious wars in France and the Low Countries, where lace making had had a long tradition, it soon became established as a traditional craft here. Over time it developed a style all of its own, with what became traditional patterns and forms distinctly different from its European predecessors. Although made all over East Devon this distinctive lace became generally known as Honiton Lace. Usually made by women and girls and very occasionally by men, young girls were introduced to the craft almost as soon as they could sit in front of a pillow.

With such a long tradition and an almost ritual introduction to the craft for all young girls it might be thought that Pat Perryman would have been part of that long tradition. Far from it, Pat came to the craft relatively late in life with no family tradition of lace making to encourage her. Born Patricia Beryl Holton in 1938, shortly before the outbreak of World War 2, her childhood was that of many young people of that time. With twin sisters following soon after her it was a busy household.

*Pat aged two and a half with her twin sisters Valerie and Carol.*
*Photographer: W.E.Berry.*

Whilst we, as children, were protected from the war by our parents, the period of austerity during and for several years after the war ensured that there was little in the way of luxuries available. Pat recalls some of the more exciting times; of joining the Guides with her smart new uniform while her younger twin sisters were 'only' Brownies. Also she remembers the excitement of enjoying a trip to the seaside at Beer when her father borrowed a horse and trap for the trip, a trip where it was necessary to walk up all the hills to spare the poor horse.

*Ready for a day at the seaside – the horse and trap taking the children to Beer.*  *Photographer: Phyllis Holton.*

Lace has always been a luxury item. The immense effort required to produce even a modest piece guaranteed this. It also guaranteed that the rewards for most lace makers were quite small, in relation to the effort put in. As a result, when lace became less fashionable and simple lace patterns could be machine made at a fraction of the cost the traditional craft of lace making began to die. There were efforts made to keep it alive with County Council sponsored lace classes, but the economics were against it. As many other hand made lace areas found, the war dealt a heavy blow to the craft and in Honiton as well as elsewhere there was a real risk of the necessary skills being lost. After the war only a few enthusiasts still practised the art and just about kept it alive.

*Sweet sixteen - Pat, the dressmaker's apprentice.*
                              Photographer: Unknown.

Pat and Derek Perryman cut the cake on their wedding day.
Photographer: Courtenay Harris.

Pat grew up knowing of Honiton lace, naturally, but with no real knowledge of, or especial interest in it. Apprenticed to a dressmaker in Exeter, dressmaking soon took second place when she met and married Derek Perryman when only 18 years old. With two young children and few of the modern labour saving devices available to today's young mothers there was little time to consider anything other than looking after the family. The dressmaking skills were very handy however and were used to good effect in earning a little 'pin' money to help the family budget. Still there was no sign of any interest in the subject that came to dominate Pat's life.

Not entirely chained to the kitchen sink, Pat had kept up her friendships with a number of local girls. In 1969 one of these friends expressed an interest in joining a Honiton Lace class, but she was too shy to go on her own. Persuaded to go along for company, while Derek looked after the children for a couple of hours, Pat could not imagine what a momentous decision she had just made. Doubly so when one considers that the class was about to close due to the lack of numbers. Pat's attendance tipped the balance and, significantly, the class continues to this day! More surprising perhaps is that the friend, Mona Collins, decided after just one lesson that unfortunately, because of eye problems, she couldn't see the prickings clearly and would not therefore be able to continue.

Perhaps because of, or maybe in spite of, her dressmaking skills it soon became apparent that Pat had a natural aptitude for the craft. Starting in the same way as she has subsequently introduced so many to the art; her first completed piece was a simple small leaf.

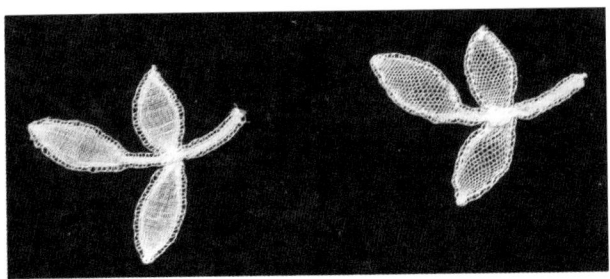

*The first two pieces of lace ever made by Pat.*
*Photographer: Trevor Hitchcock*

*The third and fourth pieces of lace made by Pat.*
*Photographer: Trevor Hitchcock.*

She quickly moved on to more complex designs and the fifth piece of lace she made was a particularly fine butterfly which clearly shows how quickly her skill as a lace maker developed. Her teacher was Mrs 'Dee' Newton who taught Honiton Lace making at the Community College here in Honiton.

*The fifth piece of lace and the first butterfly made by Pat, an early demonstration of the skill she was developing.*
*Photographer: Trevor Hitchcock.*

Pat admits that at that time she had never heard of any other kind of lace and to this day she has never felt inclined to try any other. She is totally dedicated to Honiton Lace, both in the making of it, in passing on the skills to the next generation and in preserving the finest examples from the past as part of the Allhallows Museum collection.

It was as well that Mrs Newton was a hard taskmaster. Pat's natural tendency was to make a note of and write down the instructions she had been given for future reference, but Mrs Newton would have none of it. 'Don't write it down, learn it!' became a kind of mantra. And learn it she did, so much so that only three years later in 1972 she was told that she was to become the next teacher for the class. Protesting that she had neither the knowledge nor the experience to teach, Pat was told by Mrs Newton 'the decision is made, it is my decision and that is what is going to happen'.

*Devon Lace Teachers c.1948 with standing: Mrs Whittaker, Maud Radford, Mrs 'Dee' Newton, Molly Rendell and sitting: Joyce Chambers, Mrs Tolhurst, Joan Ridge and Elsie Luxton.*
*Photographer: Unknown.*

The decision was made rather earlier than had been intended, Mrs Newton had not meant to hand over the teaching of the class for another year, but for health reasons was advised not to drive and since she lived at that time in Tedburn St Mary on the far side of Exeter there was no practical alternative. Hence Pat was thrown into the deep end as it were with no time to adjust to the idea.

It was a daunting prospect; imagine turning up to a class where many of the students had been making lace for a much longer time and having to announce 'I am your new teacher'. There was a real fear that many would get up and walk out, in the event none did. Even better, the demand for places in the class grew to the extent that the following year one class became two. A year after that there were three. By 1979 she had eighty-five pupils with students ranging from aged eleven to over seventy. This was in addition to being a tutor of Honiton Lace at Bicton College.

It was a time when craft subjects generally were being revived and in the Honiton area lace making was leading the way. The interest was phenomenal, bearing in mind that only a few brief years before the one remaining class was about to close and in fact there were very few active lace makers remaining. That such a skill might have died out doesn't bear thinking about.

Clearly there was an increasing demand and at one point Pat had seven classes running in the Honiton district alone. It was too many, what had started as an evening out with a friend had become more than a full time job. Finding that it really was too much Pat passed some of the classes on to other teachers. One hopes that their introduction to teaching the craft was a little gentler than Pat's abrupt introduction.

Several years later in conversation with Mrs Newton the subject of written notes came up, 'Why, if it helps them, shouldn't people write it down?' To Pat's surprise came the answer, 'I never minded people writing it down, but you didn't know what I knew, that you were to be the next teacher and it was vital that you learnt it and didn't just write it in a notebook.' If students today were told that they couldn't write something down the teacher would probably be told where to go!

It seems quite staggering that Mrs Newton should have been so sure, after such a short time, that she had found her successor.

At the time Pat could not imagine how she could possibly be so sure. Today, after many years of teaching, Pat says that it becomes very obvious after just a few lessons which of her students will become the best lace makers and for the special few it is clear from the very first lesson. This 'indefinable something' that some beginners have must have been seen by Mrs Newton very early on in Pat's lace making career.

In the early 1970's there were few books available on the techniques of making Honiton lace, it was very much a skill passed on by word of mouth and developed by trial and error. Later the student lace maker had much more help available with Pam Nottingham's book 'The Technique of Bobbin Lace' coming out in 1976 and Elsie Luxton's book 'The Technique of Honiton Lace' in 1979. In the 1980's further books by Elsie Luxton and Susanne Thompson gave students of lace an even wider source of reference. In 1984 Pat collaborated with Cynthia Voysey on the book which became *New Designs in Honiton Lace*. There then followed a stream of books on Honiton lace and lace making, culminating in John Yallop's book 'The History of the Honiton Lace Industry' so that today's students can relatively easily find help and illustrations in many widely available publications.

*Pat Perryman and Cynthia Voysey with the first copy of their book 'New Designs in Honiton Lace.'*   *Photographer: Unknown.*

Pat and Derek Perryman preparing for the 1975 Caen Fair.
Photographer: Unknown.

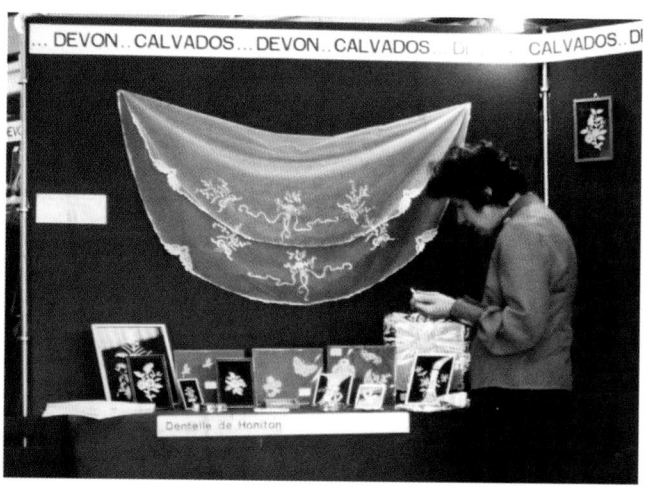

Pat Perryman at the Caen Fair in 1975.   Photographer: Unknown.

Just five years after first starting to make lace Pat was sufficiently confident and competent to demonstrate at the Ideal Homes Exhibition in London. She was approached by the National Federation of Townswomen's Guilds to demonstrate the art of Honiton Lace Making on their stand as part of their exhibit 'It's a Woman's World'.

In 1975 she went international, demonstrating at the Caen Fair in France for the first time. Devon being twinned with the Calvados Region of Normandy was exhibiting a range of traditional products and crafts from the county and Pat was invited to attend to demonstrate her skill at lace making. This very nearly didn't happen when husband Derek, who was to accompany her and use his limited French as interpreter, broke a leg just the week before the fair. Manfully he gathered up his crutches and his courage and the visit turned out to be a complete success.

Pamela Derryman and Pat Perryman at the 1979 Caen Fair.
Photographer: Unknown.

In 1978 and again in 1979 Pat was invited to once more represent Devon at the Caen Fair. Accompanied by her star pupil of the day, fifteen year old Pamela Derryman, many hundreds of people enjoyed their demonstrations. The similarity of names, Pat Perryman and Pam Derryman, caused no little confusion with some visitors convinced that they were in fact mother and daughter! Through these visits she was starting to become known internationally, a renown that has grown over the years.

Honiton lace has had a long royal connection and in 1977 Pat was honoured to make a piece of Honiton lace to be presented to the Queen from the people of Honiton in celebration of her silver jubilee. The design was of a honeysuckle entwined royal cipher ER with the dates 1952 at the top and 1977 at the bottom. Designed by Tom Griffiths, the art teacher at Honiton Secondary School, it was a beautiful piece of art in its own right, as a piece of lace it became outstanding. This was just the first of a number of important pieces of Honiton lace Pat has been associated with.

*Original Tom Griffiths drawing of his design for the Silver Jubilee lace.*                             *Photographer: Trevor Hitchcock.*

*Queen's Silver Jubilee Lace by Pat Perryman for presentation to the Queen from the people of Honiton.     Photographer: Martin Street.*

In 1981 the whole country celebrated the wedding of Prince Charles, Prince of Wales, and Lady Diana Spencer at St Paul's Cathedral in London. In honour of the occasion Pat made a fine piece of Honiton lace, depicting the Prince of Wales feathers, for presentation from the people of Honiton to the Prince and his bride as a wedding gift. Accompanied by the Honiton Town Mayor, Councillor Maurice Stone, Pat made the journey to London to deliver it to Buckingham Palace to be presented to the happy couple.

*Prince of Wales Feathers made by Pat Perryman as a Wedding gift from the people of Honiton to the Prince of Wales and Lady Diana Spencer.*　　　　*Photographer: Steve Roberts*

*The Speaker of the House of Commons Jabot designed by Tom Griffiths and made by Pat Perryman.*   *Photographer: Steve Roberts.*

At around the same time she was approached by the Member of Parliament for Honiton, Sir Peter Emery, with the suggestion that she should make a new jabot for the Speaker of the House of Commons, George Thomas. The artistic design was yet again by Tom Griffiths, art teacher at the Honiton Secondary School; he claimed that he doodled the basic design while sitting in a very boring staff meeting at the College. It was a complex design with a great deal of symbolism. One face shows the crown and portcullis of the House of Commons emblem supported by the flowers of the four countries of the United Kingdom, the rose, thistle, shamrock and daffodil. The other face shows, in the centre, a stylised view of Dumpdon Hill, which sits just to the north-east of Honiton, supported on each side by an otter, the River Otter forming the northern boundary of Honiton, each otter is holding a small fish. These are separated by sprigs of honeysuckle as a symbol of Honiton. If you look very carefully you can see that the piece is signed PP and has the dates between which it was made incorporated into the design. This piece took many hundreds of hours work to complete, over about three years, by which time there was a new Speaker of the House.

*Detail of the lace on the Speaker of the House of Commons jabot showing the Shamrock and Thistle.*     *Photographer: Steve Roberts.*

*Detail of the lace on the Speaker of the House of Commons Jabot showing the Rose and Daffodil.*   *Photographer: Steve Roberts.*

To add to the workload it was decided at the same time to make a new jabot for the Mayor of Honiton. After preparing the basic design Pat organised local lace makers from her classes to make the new jabot. It was a big communal undertaking with many local lace makers contributing, with the aggregate number of hours for the work exceeding 300. It was gifted to the town by the lace makers of Honiton and is regularly worn by the Town Mayor on ceremonial occasions. The jabot was first worn by Councillor Arthur Dimond, Town Mayor, when he led the Honiton Carnival parade of October 1982.

The day when the Rt. Hon. Bernard Weatherill, P.C., M.P., Speaker of the House of Commons came to Honiton to be presented with the new lace jabot was described by the local press as 'the biggest day since the visit of King Charles in 1644'. As well as the formal presentation, for the first time in nearly a century the town witnessed a parade of lace makers. Many local people are proud to recall the twenty-third of June 1984 when Honiton lace makers entertained the Speaker of the House of Commons. Lace making in Honiton had come a long way since the evening when Pat was persuaded to go along for company, and nearly a hundred lace makers proudly paraded through the town. Dressed in long black skirts with two pairs of bobbins attached to the waistband and white blouses, each lace maker carried a white wand topped with flowers and the ladies leading the procession carried a large banner, worked in lace, proclaiming 'The Honiton Lace makers'. This was the first recorded parade of Lace Makers in the town since Queen Victoria's Golden Jubilee in 1887. The earliest record of a lace makers' parade dates from 1702 when three hundred women and girls are said to have marched to celebrate the coronation of Queen Anne. Later in the eighteenth century reports speak of an annual parade, but by the nineteenth century such gatherings seem to have become rarer and only occurred on very special occasions. The presentation to the Speaker of a new jabot was a very special occasion in Honiton and worthy of such a parade.

*Pat leading the Honiton Lace Makers' Parade.*

*Photographer: Unknown.*

After the parade, from Allhallows Museum down the High Street and along Dowell Street, to the Royal British Legion Club came the formal presentation to the Speaker of the new jabot.

*Presentation to the Speaker of the new Jabot.*
*Photographer: Unknown.*

In the presence of the Town Mayor, Councillor Pat Allen, the Member of Parliament for Honiton, Sir Peter Emery, Freeman of the Borough of Honiton, F.W.C. (Bill) Tucker and other local dignitaries, Pat was proud to present the Speaker with the new jabot. After the formal ceremonies the Speaker and his wife, accompanied by Pat, were driven by Alec Parris in his 1926 open-topped car to the New Dolphin Hotel for a civic luncheon.

*The Speaker leaves the Royal British Legion Club.*
*Photographer: Unknown.*

To complete the day's festivities the Speaker unveiled a commemorative plaque, specially crafted by the Honiton Pottery, in Allhallows Museum.

*Commemorative Plaque unveiled in Allhallows Museum by the Speaker, Bernard Weatherill with Rachel Yallop, John Yallop (Museum Curator), and Pat Allen (Mayor). Photographer: Unknown.*

*The Speaker Bernard Weatherill meets Paul Redvers of the Honiton Pottery and Rachel Yallop, (designer of the Plaque).*
*Photographer: Unknown.*

The following November Pat was invited to the State Opening of Parliament to see the Speaker wearing the new jabot. The Speaker, the Rt. Hon. Bernard Weatherill, P.C., M.P., had expressed the wish that Pat be there when he wore the lace for the very first time in an official capacity. It was a proud moment in Pat's life, photographed with the Speaker in full regalia and at the reception, in the company of Sir Peter Emery, MP for Honiton, and Councillor Pat Allen, Honiton Town Mayor, meeting the Prime Minister, Margaret Thatcher, and other government ministers and leading politicians.

*State Opening of Parliament, Peter Emery M.P., Pat Perryman, Bernard Weatherill P.C., M.P. (the Speaker), Pat Allen (Honiton Town Mayor) and John Yallop (Curator of Allhallows Museum).*
*Photographer: Colin Bowerman.*

During the reception, while drinking copious amounts of House of Commons champagne, (after all the opportunity doesn't occur very often), Pat was rather taken aback when asked if she could make a pair of cuffs to match the jabot. 'Well, it will take some time,' she replied and the next major project had been decided upon.

One of the Speaker's Cuffs on the pillow.    Photographer: Unknown.

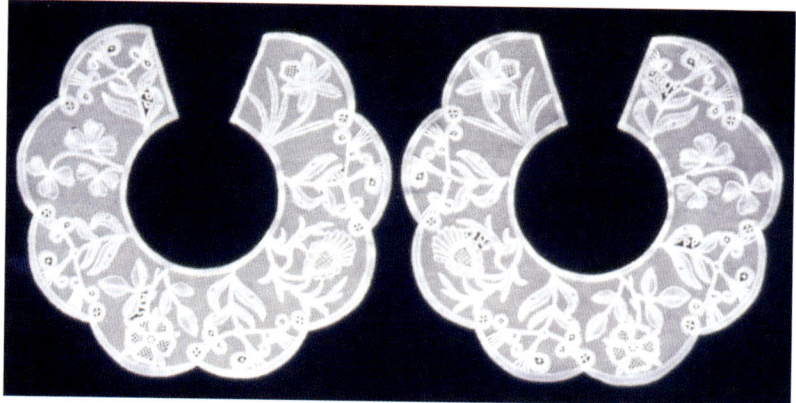

The pair of finished cuffs.    Photographer: Unknown.

It took even longer than she had first thought with each cuff requiring around five hundred hours of detailed and painstaking work to complete. The design was based on that of part of the jabot showing the flowers of the four countries of the United Kingdom with each separated by a sprig of honeysuckle.

It was almost four years and a thousand hours of work before the cuffs were complete. Each cuff is a mirror image of the other and is signed 'PP' as well as having the dates between which it was made incorporated into the design. The more observant may note that these are not an exact mirror image as the dates and signature are in different places on the different cuffs. Finally in 1989 they were complete and could be presented to the Speaker at an exhibition of lace and needlework entitled 'Lace as Art.' The Prix Betonac Exhibition being held in the Fairfield Halls in Croydon, where Bernard Weatherill was the local M.P.

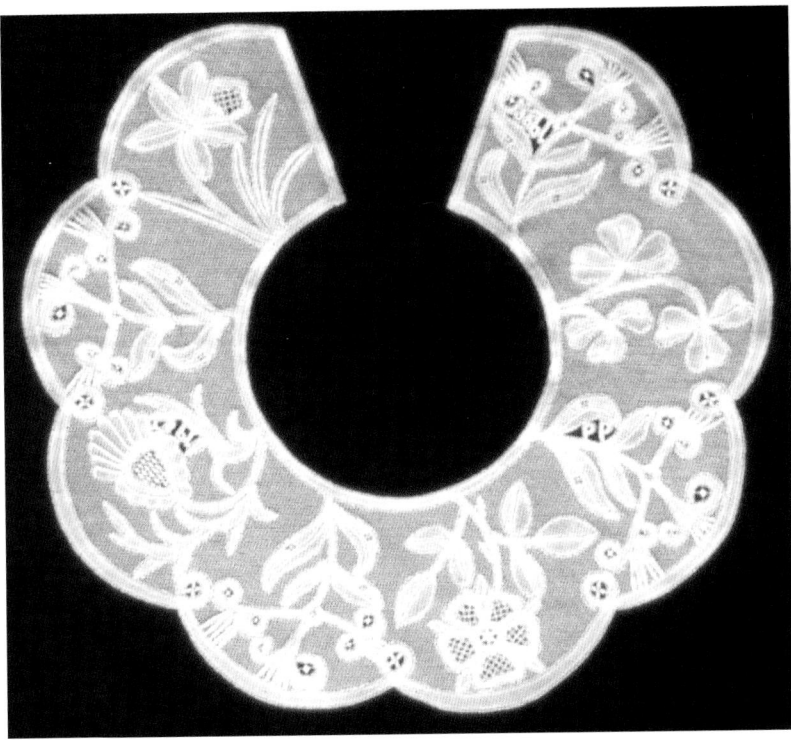

*One of the pair of cuffs made for the Speaker of the House of Commons by Pat Perryman. (Note the PP signature and the date incorporated into the design.)*          *Photographer: unknown.*

*The Presentation of the Cuffs to the Speaker at Croydon.*
*Photographer: Mary Wardell.*

The 1980's were quite hectic for Pat and showed just how much lace making had taken over her life. In a dozen years or so what began as a potential hobby had become the dominant force in her life. To describe it as an obsession is possibly an overstatement, but it is also not too far from the truth. The chain to the kitchen sink had long been broken, now she had become entangled in the web of Honiton Lace to the benefit of us all.

In addition to making significantly important pieces of lace for the Royal wedding and the jabot and cuffs for the Speaker, she also served on the Lace Guild Executive Committee for three years, all the while teaching several lace classes locally as well as teaching at the Royal School of Needlework. In 1980 she won a competition for a piece of lace suitable for a Christmas card. From an entry of forty her Madonna and Child design was selected by the Lace Guild which produced some 20,000 cards to her winning design. In 1984 the collected patterns of Pat's lace were published by Allhallows Museum in Honiton as 'Pat Perryman's Lace Patterns'. Twenty five years later these are still in great demand.

*Madonna and Child, Designed and Made by Pat Perryman – Winner of a Christmas card Design Competition run by the Lace Guild.*   *Photographer: Margaret Lewis.*

In 1982 she was instrumental in organising the first Honiton Lace Day which attracted 300 visitors from all over the country. This was so successful that it became an annual event. It was inspired by a need to raise funds to support the children's lace making classes after the County Council withdrew all funding for this. Over the following years sufficient funds have been raised to subsidise the classes and leave a five figure surplus which the lace makers have used to buy significant pieces of lace that were subsequently donated to Allhallows Museum and form part of their extensive collection.

*An early Honiton Lace Day.*     Photographer: Unknown.

Obviously inspired by the 1984 parade of lace makers in Honiton to celebrate the visit of the Speaker of the House of Commons, when the Speaker's jabot was presented, a similar parade was organised in 1987 in Exeter to celebrate the opening of Rougemont House as a Museum of Costume and Lace. Pat was again involved, together with the Devon Lace Teachers, and on $22^{nd}$ August over one hundred and fifty lace makers in long black skirts and white blouses carrying flower bedecked white staffs gathered outside the west front of the Cathedral.

*Honiton Lace Makers gathering by the west front of Exeter Cathedral, Pat Perryman with John Yallop, curator of Allhallows Museum.*                       *Photographer: Unknown.*

Jean Hooper, one of the ladies taking part in this historic event, described the occasion: '*Our eminent teacher Pat Perryman resplendent in her black dress with beautiful Honiton Lace collar and flounce, summoned us to our positions, today though with a variation on the theme of one to the right, two to the left, one to the right, twist three, don't forget your pin and make up your edge. We lined up with partners of the same height, the shortest leading the procession.*' From the Cathedral green they moved up the High Street to the ancient Guildhall with Pat at their head, two of their number carrying the Honiton Lace Maker's banner.

*Lace Makers prepare to leave the Cathedral Green for the formal Parade.*  *Photographer: Unknown.*

*Parade of Lace Makers passing along Exeter High Street with Pat Perryman at their head.*  *Photographer: Unknown.*

Then, she continues: '*With our banner held high we set off, to be led from the Guildhall (the oldest municipal building in England) by the Lympstone Town Band and the Mayor of Exeter, resplendent in his chain of office and travelling in his white Rolls-Royce.*' The Parade passed along the High Street and into Castle Street to Rougemont House and Gardens. The event was blessed with fine weather and made a great spectacle in the city, reminding everyone of the importance of the textile industry in Exeter's past and that through lace the connection was still alive. Today, only a few years later, the Rougemont House Museum of Costume and Lace has been absorbed into Exeter's Royal Albert Memorial Museum.

Teaching lace making had taken a great deal of Pat's time, but it seemed that there was still time for another activity and gradually she became ever more involved with Allhallows Museum in Honiton. She first gave a demonstration of lace making at Allhallows Museum in 1973 but in 1980 was invited by the museum curator, John Yallop, to demonstrate regularly at the museum for one afternoon a week; she was soon joined by Jackie Ford. This was the beginning of a long relationship with Allhallows Museum and also the start of the regular demonstrations, by many volunteers, of Honiton Lace Making which are given at the museum throughout the summer months.

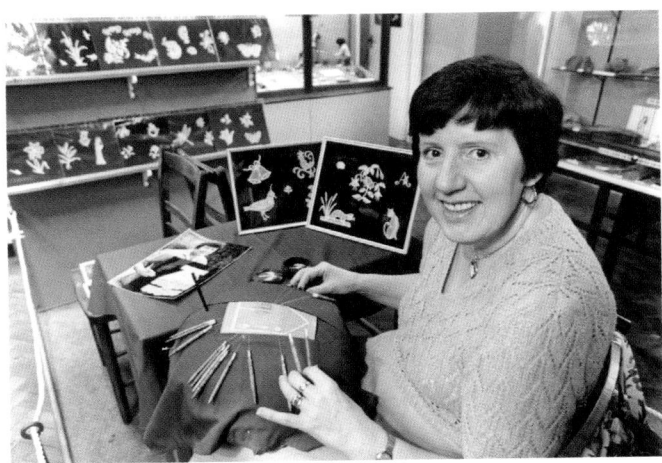

An early Lace Making Demonstration at Allhallows Museum, Honiton.   Photographer: Unknown.

From demonstrating the art of making Honiton Lace she moved on to assisting Mary Yallop, Keeper of Textiles, at the museum; then gradually her interest and expertise in the making of Honiton Lace ensured that she became more and more involved with the lace collection. Pat Earnshaw was the original lace advisor to the museum, being called in as and when required. At that time the museum collection was very limited with no more than a couple of dozen pieces, since then it has grown to around 2000 including many of the best and most important pieces of Honiton Lace ever made. In 1995 Pat became the museum's official Keeper of Lace. Then in 2003 after a number of years as a committee member she became the Museum Chairman.

The first success as Museum Chairman came when Phil Harding of Channel 4's 'Time Team' was persuaded by Mary Wardell to come to Honiton and give a talk about his career in archaeology. This was heavily oversubscribed and it is probable that the hall at the Community College could have been filled twice over. This event gave a welcome boost to the Museum finances.

Allhallows Museum was honoured by a visit in 2005 from Princess Anne, the Princess Royal and Pat was proud to show our royal guest around the museum, to show her many of the exhibits and introduce the museum volunteers.

*H.R.H. Princess Anne being introduced to museum volunteers Donna Lewis and Trevor Hitchcock by Pat Perryman and Margaret Lewis.*
*Photographer: Colin Bowerman.*

At the end of the royal visit Pat was pleased to present the Princess with a piece of Honiton Lace showing a swan alighting on a lake as a memento of the Princess's visit to Honiton.

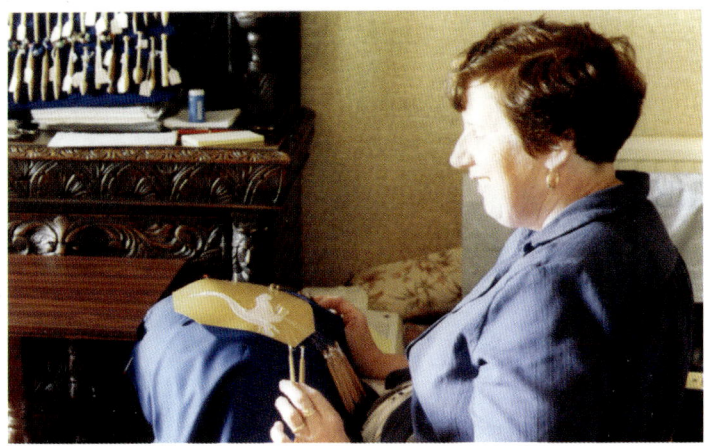

*Pat Perryman working on the lace swan for later presentation to H.R.H. Princess Anne.* *Photographer: Unknown.*

*Lace piece made by Pat Perryman and presented to H.R.H. Princess Anne to commemorate her visit to Allhallows Museum 11th April 2005.* *Photographer: Margaret Lewis.*

# HONITON TOWN COUNCIL

*At a meeting of Honiton Town Council held on the fourteenth day of February, 2005*

The Town Mayor and Councillors of Honiton Town Council, on behalf of the inhabitants of Honiton

**RESOLVED**
to confer the title of

## Honoured Citizen
upon

### Mrs Patricia Beryl Perryman

in appreciation and recognition of the eminent and devoted services rendered by her over many years to the people and Town of Honiton

*Sally Cann*
COUNCILLOR MRS S.A. CASSON
TOWN MAYOR OF HONITON

*John Spencer*
MR J.P. SPENCER
TOWN CLERK

Certificate awarded to Pat Perryman by the Honiton Town Council and presented to her by H.R.H. Princess Anne.

Photographer: Margaret Lewis.

On the same occasion Pat herself was honoured when she was presented by the Princess Royal with an 'Honoured Citizen' certificate awarded by the Honiton Town Council in recognition of her work as a lace maker and in promoting Honiton and Honiton lace throughout the world.

H.R.H. Princess Anne presents an 'Honoured Citizen' award on behalf of the Honiton Town Council to Pat Perryman while John Spencer, (Town Clerk) and Sally Casson, (Town Mayor) look on.
Photographer: Colin Bowerman.

Allhallows Museum has probably the world's finest collection of Honiton Lace with pieces known to date from as early as 1590. Each year about one third of the displays of lace are changed, this is to enable as much of the collection as possible to be displayed over time. The collection is not restricted solely to Honiton Lace, though naturally enough it forms the bulk of the collection, select examples of other laces are always on display for comparison. In addition, as well as a short video about lace making continuously showing, for many years Pat has organised a rota of lace makers from her classes to attend and demonstrate the art in the museum during the summer months. These are all volunteers, indeed the museum is entirely run by volunteers, who willingly give their time and skills for the enjoyment of visitors.

One of the modern highlights of the lace collection is the splendid Millennium Christening Robe with bonnet and bib designed by Joan Beckett and made by 27 local ladies, including Pat Perryman. All of the ladies who contributed to the making of this fine piece have the right to borrow it for their family Christenings; at the time of writing it has been used four times. The first child to wear the robe at their Christening was the grand-daughter of Val and Howard Foss. Hannah Lucy Mae Dunwoody was baptised by her grandfather in October 2004 at Farway, where her father, Stephen Dunwoody, was then Rector. The Christening robe is quite charming with a design incorporating the flowers and foliage of the typical Devon hedgerow. This splendid piece of work shows that the skills that made the name of Honiton Lace famous throughout the world are still to be found in the locality.

*First use of the Millennium Christening Robe by Hannah Dunwoody. Picture shows: Val Foss (Hannah's grandmother), Mary Wardell, Hannah, Rev. John Connell, Pat Perryman and Joan Beckett (Designer of the robe).*

*Photographer: Howard Foss.*

*Harebell Flower Fairy by Pat Perryman.*
*Photographer: Trevor Hitchcock.*

*Cowslip Flower Fairy by Pat Perryman.*

*Photographer: Trevor Hitchcock.*

*Lily of the Valley Flower Fairy by Pat Perryman.*
*Photographer: Trevor Hitchcock.*

*Primrose Flower Fairy by Pat Perryman.*

*Photographer: Trevor Hitchcock.*

From time to time the museum has exhibited pieces of Pat's lace. The twelve lace ladies were especial favourites of our visitors. As a result the patterns are now available from the museum shop as the 'Twelve periods of Fashion'. These all have suitable names and cover the various fashions from around 1400 to the 1920's. Starting with Berengaria 1400 and following on with Guinivere 1450, Eleanor 1500, Kathrine 1550, Elizabeth 1600, Beatrice 1650, Isabella 1700, Charlotte 1750, Sophia 1800, Victoria 1850, Roseina 1900 and finishing with Angela 1920. Each piece depicts a lady dressed in the typical fashion of her time.

Since becoming chairman of the Museum Trustees Pat has still found plenty of time for lace making and has completed a set of four Flower Fairies. Each fairy carries a different flower, primrose, harebell, cowslip and lily of the valley. These are available from the museum as a set of postcards. She also managed to find time to respond to a request to make a jabot for Martin Edmunds Q.C.

It seems that butterflies are very popular and the stewards are frequently asked if the museum shop has any lace incorporating a butterfly design for sale. Sadly, all too often the answer is no. Over the years Pat has frequently returned to the butterfly theme for the design of the lace she is making, in fact the fifth piece of lace she ever made depicts a butterfly and in 2008 she completed a lace parasol incorporating twenty-four butterflies each of a different design.

*Pat with Butterfly Parasol.*  *Photographer: Margaret Lewis.*

*Group of students for lace week at Honiton with Mary Bolshaw, (back row 3$^{rd}$ from left), Trevor Bolshaw, (back row centre) and Pat Perryman, (seated on wall at right).*  *Photographer: Unknown.*

*Group of students for lace week at Honiton with Pat Perryman seated 4$^{th}$ from left.*  *Photographer: Unknown.*

Starting in 1975 when, representing the County of Devon, she first demonstrated the art of Honiton Lace making at the Caen Fair in France, her overseas trips have become ever more frequent. At first they were rare and very low key events and for quite small groups and involved demonstrating rather than teaching. As she became better known, people began to come to Honiton to avail themselves of the opportunity to join Pat's lace class for a day or a week. This in turn led to regular weekend schools and even lace weeks especially to cater to the world at large rather than just those who lived locally. With Mary Bolshaw providing the food and some accommodation for the residential schools and Mary's husband Trevor some splendid musical accompaniment, places were eagerly sought. With numbers restricted to a maximum of eighteen on each course it was soon found to be not enough and demands were such that classes were organised around the country where Pat would demonstrate and teach the enthusiasts in their own local areas.

The following year (1976) she had her first foreign student, Kay Asahi, from California, USA, who strange as it may seem was actually Japanese! Since then she has had many more overseas visitors coming to Honiton for her lace making classes. One of her more notable students was her younger sister Carol, now living in Australia, who on a rare visit back to Honiton was taught by Pat and is now a respected lace maker in Australia. Having had students attend courses in Honiton from Australia, Belgium, Canada, France, Holland, Japan and the USA, among others, it was logical to start giving classes overseas.

The first formal overseas class was held in 1992 at Ithaca in New York State, U.S.A. It was such a success that Pat has been invited back on more than one occasion, each time to meet a yet larger group. She has also been invited to teach in Belgium, France, Germany, Spain and Switzerland as well as the U.S.A. There is still time for a few more countries to be added to the list in the coming years.

The demand for these courses, both in the U.K. and overseas, has become such that few weeks pass without a trip away from Honiton to teach, talk about or demonstrate the art of making Honiton Lace. Increasingly Pat has had to become more discriminating over how many and what type of event she takes on. At times husband Derek must feel like a 'Lace Widow' as Pat sets off once more to yet another faraway destination.

*Pat with a group of her students in Switzerland.*
*Photographer: Unknown.*

*Pat with a group of her students in Brussels, Belgium.*
*Photographer: Unknown.*

*Pat with a children's lace making class, c.1980.*
*Photographer: Unknown.*

The work she has done in teaching and promoting the art of Honiton Lace making to both children and adults over forty years has in a large part kept the skill alive in the Town that gave the craft its name. The intense workload and commitment necessary to maintain such an active programme of classes, demonstrations and talks could not go on forever and in 2001 when a double hip replacement became necessary she was out of action for several weeks. It was clearly time to review her schedule. During this time Wendy Williams took charge of the children's lace making class, as Pat put it; 'I couldn't move around and things can be quite hectic with kiddiewinks.' Wendy would understand as just a few years earlier she had been one of those 'kiddiewinks'. After a couple of months, during which Wendy successfully looked after the children's class, it was obvious that part of the solution had been found. Wendy would look after the children while Pat carried on with the adult classes. It must have been quite a satisfying moment for both of them when the former pupil became the teacher.

*Three generations of the Meyer family, Sarah-Louise, Tanith and Margaret practice the art at Pat's lace class.*
*Photographer: Margaret Lewis.*

Passing on the children's class to another has not entirely severed Pat's links with the children; each year Allhallows Museum sponsors a Children's Lace Making Competition with Pat as one of the judges.

*Presentation to Shannon Norman and Jessica Moss, winners of the 2004 Children's Lace Making competition, by Town Mayor, Sally Casson with teachers Wendy Williams and Pat Perryman.*
*Photographer: Margaret Lewis.*

*Examples of children's work from the 2007 competition on display in Allhallows Museum.*   *Photographer: Trevor Hitchcock.*

It is very gratifying to see the high quality of work produced by these local children, some of whom are happy, during school holiday times, to demonstrate their art to visitors in the museum. Many are amazed by the skill and knowledge displayed by these young ladies which is a tribute to both their enthusiasm and the skill and patience of their lace teachers.

In the winter 2008 edition of *East Devon Views* the museum's two youngest volunteers, Bethany Sillitoe aged 13 and Rowanne Small aged 12 were featured as a sign of the success of the children's lace making classes and an indication that the future of lace making in Honiton was in good hands. All the indications are that when Pat finally puts aside her pillow and hangs up her bobbins there will be skilled and enthusiastic lace makers ready to take her place. That there are is in no small part due to the enthusiasm and dedication Pat has put to the craft since that evening forty years ago when she went along to her first class, 'just for company'.

*Pat with Allhallows Museum's youngest volunteers Bethany Sillitoe and Rowanne Small.*

*Photographer: Belinda Bennett.*

There is no sign yet that Pat is ready to put away her pillow though she does feel that it is time that she lightened the load a little. Having passed the children's classes over to Wendy Williams she has also had to cut back slightly on the residential courses in Honiton and after much thought has decided that organisation of the Lace Day is becoming rather too demanding. Hopefully some one else can be persuaded to keep it going, if not annually then at least biennially. The finance of course to keep the children's lace classes viable is still very much needed and the Honiton Lace Makers have been hard at work with alternative fund raising events to ensure these classes can continue.

This small volume is one non lace maker's tribute to a lady who has dedicated much of her life to Honiton Lace. The many hundreds of lace makers who have benefited from Pat's teaching and have been encouraged to hone their skills in the ancient craft would, I'm sure, join me in saying, 'well done Pat.'

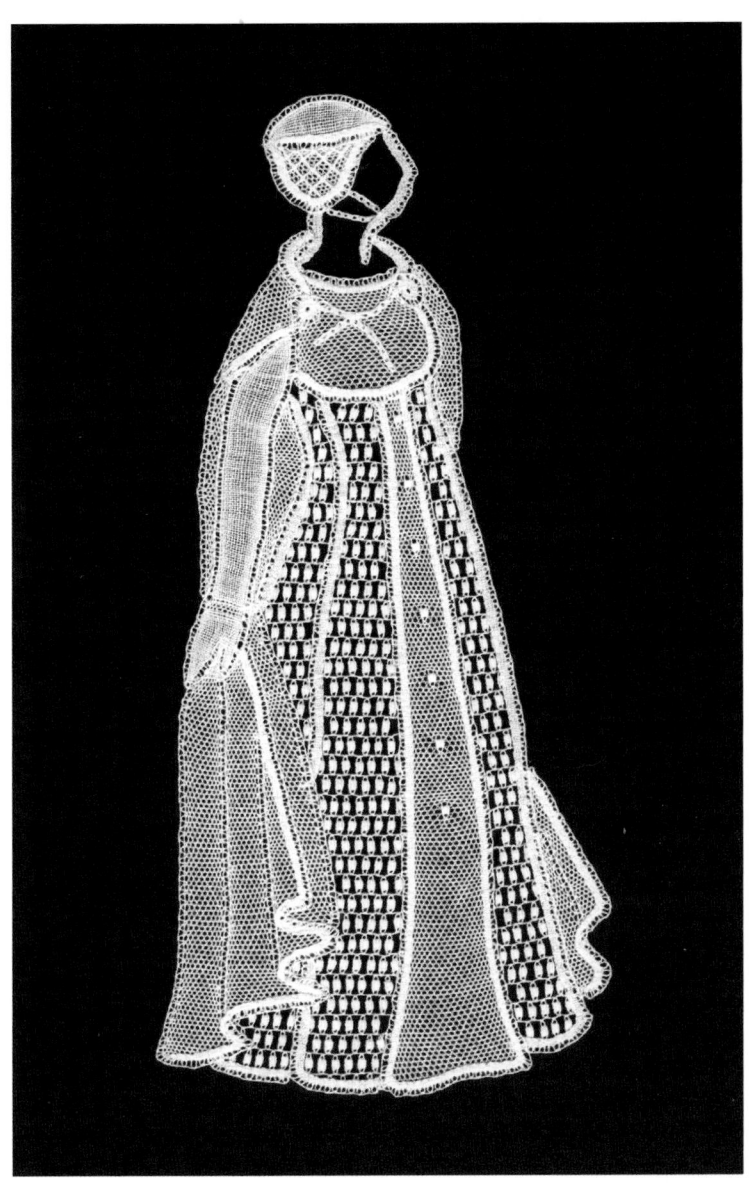

*Number 1 of Twelve Ladies of Fashion -* Berengaria 1400
*Photographer: Trevor Hitchcock.*

*Number 2 of Twelve Ladies of Fashion - Guinivere 1450*
*Photographer: Trevor Hitchcock.*

*Number 3 of Twelve Ladies of Fashion - Eleanor 1500*
*Photographer: Trevor Hitchcock.*

Number 4 of Twelve Ladies of Fashion - *Kathrine 1550*
Photographer: Trevor Hitchcock.

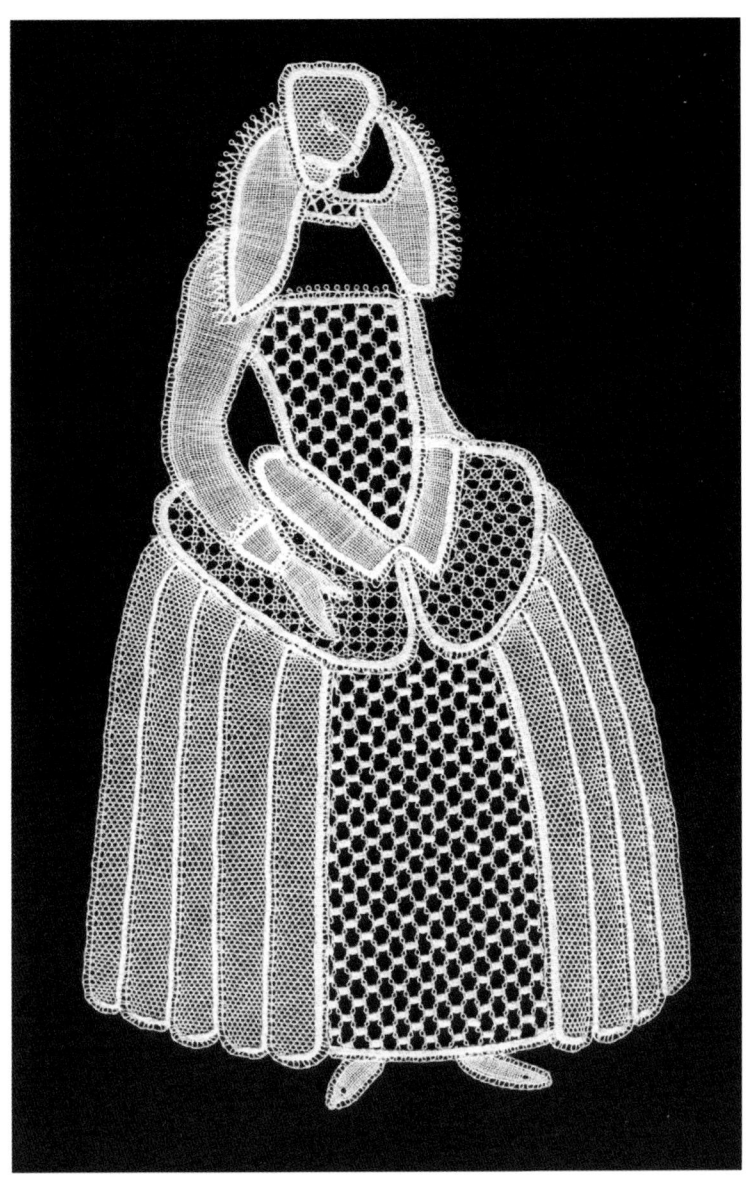

*Number 5 of Twelve Ladies of Fashion - Elizabeth 1600*
*Photographer: Trevor Hitchcock.*

Number 6 of Twelve Ladies of Fashion - *Beatrice 1650*
Photographer: Trevor Hitchcock.

Number 7 of Twelve Ladies of Fashion - *Isabella 1700*
Photographer: Trevor Hitchcock.

Number 8 of Twelve Ladies of Fashion - *Charlotte 1750*
Photographer: Trevor Hitchcock.

Number 9 of Twelve Ladies of Fashion - *Sophia 1800*
Photographer: Trevor Hitchcock.

Number 10 of Twelve Ladies of Fashion - *Victoria 1850*
Photographer: Trevor Hitchcock.

Number 11 of Twelve Ladies of Fashion - *Roseina 1900*
Photographer: Trevor Hitchcock.

*Number 12 of Twelve Ladies of Fashion - Angela 1920*
*Photographer: Trevor Hitchcock.*

# Bibliography

**'The Technique of Bobbin Lace'** by Pamela Nottingham. Published by Batsford Books, 1975.

**'The Technique of Honiton Lace'** by Elsie Luxton. Published by Batsford Books, 1979.

**'Honiton Lace Patterns'** by Elsie Luxton. Published by Batsford Books, 1983.

**'New Designs in Honiton Lace'** by Pat Perryman and Cynthia Voysey. Published by Batsford Books, 1984.

**'Introduction to Honiton Lace'** by Susanne Thompson. Published by Batsford Books, 1985.

**'Honiton Lace – The Visual Approach'** by Elsie Luxton and Yusai Fukuyama. Published by Batsford Books, 1988.

**'Royal Honiton Lace'** by Elsie Luxton and Yusai Fukuyama. Published by Batsford Books, 1988.

**'Honiton Lace – A Practical Guide'** by Cynthia Voysey. Published by Bishopsgate Press, 1991.

**'Flowers in Honiton Lace'** by Elsie Luxton and Yusai Fukuyama. Published by Batsford Books, 1992.

**'The History of the Honiton Lace Industry'** by John Yallop. Published by Exeter University Press, 1992.

**'Birds and Animals in Honiton Lace'** by Saikoh Takano. Published by Batsford Books, 1992.

**'New Patterns in Honiton Lace'** by Caroline and Barry Biggins. Published by Batsford Books, 1993.

**'Honiton Lace – basic technical instruction book'** by Joyce Dorsett. Published by The Lace Guild, 1996.

# Index

## A
Allen, Pat.  20, 21, 22
Anne, Princess.  31, 32, 33, 34
Anne, Queen.  19
Asahi, Kay.  42

## B
Beckett, Joan.  35
Bennett, Belinda.  47
Berry, W.E.  2
Bibliography.  60
Bicton College.  9
Bolshaw, Mary.  41, 42
Bolshaw, Trevor.  41, 42
Bowerman, Colin.  31, 34
Butterfly Lace.  7, 40
Butterfly Parasol.  40

## C
Caen Fair.  11, 12, 42
Casson, Sally.  34, 45
Chambers, Joyce.  8
Charles and Diana Lace.  15, 25
Charles, King.  18
Charles, Prince of Wales.  15
Children's Lace Making.  44 to 47
Christening Robe.  35
Christmas card design.  25, 26
Collins, Mona,  6
Connell, Rev. John.  35
Cuffs, Speaker's.  22 to 25

## D
Derryman, Pamela.  12, 13
Dimond, Arthur.  18
Dunwoody, Hannah.  35
Dunwoody, Rev. Stephen.  35

## E
Earnshaw, Pat.  31
Edmunds, Martin.  40
Emery, Sir Peter.  17, 20, 22

## F
Flower Fairies.  36 to 40
Ford, Jackie.  30
Foss, Howard.  35
Foss, Val.  35

## G
Griffiths, Tom. 13, 16, 17
## H
Harding, Phil. 31
Harris, Courtenay. 5
Hitchcock, Trevor. 31
Holton, Carol. 1, 2, 42
Holton, Harry. 1
Holton, Patricia B. 2
Holton, Phyllis. 3
Holton, Valerie. 1, 2
Honiton Lace Day. 27, 47
Honiton Lace makers. 18, 19, 28, 29, 47
Honoured Citizen Award. 33, 34
Hooper, Jean. 28
## I
Ideal Homes Exhibition. 12
## J
Jabot, Honiton Mayor's. 18
Jabot, Speaker's. 16 to 20, 22, 25
## L
Lace Guild. 25, 26
Lace Ladies (12 periods of fashion). 40, 48 to 59
Lewis, Donna. 31
Lewis, Margaret. 26, 31, 32, 33, 40, 45
Luxton, Elsie. 8, 10
Lympstone Town Band. 29
## M
Madonna and Child Lace. 25, 26
Meyer, Margaret. 45
Meyer, Sarah-Louise. 45
Meyer, Tanith. 45
Millennium Christening Robe. 35
Moss, Jessica. 45
## N
Newton, Mrs 'Dee'. 7, 8, 9, 10
Norman, Shannon. 45
Nottingham, Pam. 10
## P
Parliament, State Opening. 22
Parris, Alec. 20
Perryman, Derek. 5, 6, 11, 12, 43
Perryman, Graham. 64
Perryman, Suzette. 64
Pottery, Honiton. 21

## P
Prince of Wales Feathers. 15
Prix Betonac Exhibition. 24

## Q
Queen's Silver Jubilee Lace. 13, 14
Queen Anne. 19

## R
Radford, Maud. 8
Redvers, Paul. 21
Rendell, Molly. 8
Richards, Siobhan. 46
Ridge, Joan. 8
Roberts, Steve. 15, 16, 17, 18
Rougemont House Museum. 27
Royal British Legion Club. 19, 20
Royal School of Needlework. 25

## S
Sillitoe, Bethany. 46, 47
Small, Rowanne. 46, 47
Spencer, John. 34
Spencer, Lady Diana. 15
Stone, Maurice. 15
Street, Martin. 14
Swan, Lace. 32

## T
Thatcher, Margaret. 22
Thomas, George. 17
Thompson, Susanne. 10
Tolhurst, Mrs. 8
Townswomen's Guilds. 12
Tucker, F.W.C. (Bill). 20

## V
Victoria, Queen. 19
Voysey, Cynthia. 10

## W
Wardell, Mary. 25, 35
Weatherill, Bernard. 18, 21, 22, 24
Whittaker, Mrs. 8
Williams, Wendy. 44, 45, 47

## Y
Yallop, John. 10, 21, 22, 28, 30
Yallop, Mary. 31
Yallop, Rachel. 21